THE KETOGENIC DIARY

Everything you need to know about the ketoogenic diet: how to lose weight without stress, including healthy and organic sumptuous meals like keto smoothies, fat bombs, soups, etc

COPYRIGHT

Email:stjoefrances@gmail.com

Contents

<u>WHAT IS KETO DIET?</u>

Keto diet (Ketogenic diet) is a low-carb diet with a high percentage of fat in the diet, in which the body produces ketones in the liver and uses them as energy.
Initially, the main most familiar and accessible source of energy for our body is glucose. Which happens when you eat something high in carbohydrates, our body processes them into glucose, which increases the blood sugar and for its stabilization and the distribution of glucose in the cells of the body, in which the pancreas produces insulin.
Glucose is the simplest molecule in our body that is converted and used as energy, so it will be chosen over any other source of energy.
Insulin is produced to process glucose in the blood by moving it throughout the body.
The ultimate goal of the keto diet is to switch us to the state of ketosis. It is important to understand that it does not start with a low-calorie intake, but with

low carbohydrate content in the diet.

Our bodies are incredibly adaptive as soon as they lack glucose; they easily switch to ketosis and begin to use fats as the main source of energy.

DIFFERENT TYPES OF KETOGENIC DIETS

There are several versions of the ketogenic diet, including:

- **Standard ketogenic diet (SKD):** This is a very low-carb, moderate-protein and high-fat diet. It typically contains 75% fat, 20% protein and only 5% carbs

- **Cyclical ketogenic diet (CKD):** This diet involves periods of higher-carb refeeds, such as 5 ketogenic days followed by 2 high-carb days. That is to say, 5 days on the ketogenic diet and two days off which allows you eat carbs.

- **Targeted ketogenic diet (TKD):** This diet allows you to add carbs around workouts. The TKD is mainly used by the sports people.

- **High-protein ketogenic diet:** This is similar to a standard ketogenic diet, but includes more protein. The ratio is often 60% fat, 35% protein and 5% carbs. However, only the standard and high-protein ketogenic diets have been studied extensively. Cyclical or targeted ketogenic diets are more advanced methods and primarily used by bodybuilders or athletes.

<u>BENEFITS OF KETO DIET</u>

- **Ketogenic diets can help you lose weight:** A ketogenic diet is an effective way to lose weight and lower risk factors for disease. In fact, research shows that the ketogenic diet is far superior to the often recommended. What's more, the diet is so filling that you can lose weight without counting calories or tracking your food intake.

A research study found that people on a ketogenic diet lost 2.2 times more weight than those on a calorie-restricted low-fat diet.

There are several reasons why a ketogenic diet is superior to a low-fat diet, including the increased protein intake, which provides numerous benefits:

The increased ketones, lower blood sugar levels and improved insulin sensitivity may also play a key role

The ketogenic diet actually originated as a tool for treating neurological diseases such as epilepsy.

Studies have now shown that the diet can have benefits for a wide variety of different health conditions:

- **Heart disease:** The ketogenic diet can improve risk factors like body fat, HDL cholesterol levels, blood pressure and blood sugar
- **Cancer:** The diet is currently being used to treat several types of cancer and slow tumor growth
- **Alzheimer's disease:** The keto diet may reduce symptoms of Alzheimer's disease and slow its progression
- **Epilepsy:** Research has shown that the ketogenic diet can cause massive reductions in seizures in epileptic children.
- **Parkinson's disease:** One study found that the diet helped improve symptoms of Parkinson's disease.

- **Polycystic ovary syndrome:** The ketogenic diet can help reduce insulin levels, which may play a key role in polycystic ovary syndrome

- **Brain injuries:** One study found that the diet can reduce concussions and aid recovery after brain injury

- **Acne:** Lower insulin levels and eating less sugar or processed foods may help improve acne

<u>THE KETO FLU AND HOW TO AVOID IT.</u>

Although the ketogenic diet is safe for healthy people, there may be some initial side effects while your body adapts. This is often referred to as the **KETO FLU** and is usually over within a few days.

Keto flu includes poor energy and mental function, increased hunger, headaches, sleep issues, nausea, digestive discomfort and decreased exercise performance. Craving for sugar, dizziness, Irritability, Fog in the head, Poor concentration, Stomach pain, Cramps, and Muscle soreness.

But don't be scared, don't panic it's only for a few days.

To minimize this, you can try a regular low-carb diet for the first few weeks. This may teach your body to burn more fat before you completely eliminate carbs. A ketogenic diet can also change the water and mineral balance of your body, so adding extra salt to your meals or taking supplements can help like taking bullet proof coffee. Keto flu is not a virus that infects only those who decide to try a ketogenic diet.

<u>THE KETO FLU REMEDIES</u>

1. Drink more water (with a pinch of unrefined salt). Hydration is vital, especially when you are on a ketogenic diet. If during a keto diet you do not drink enough water, you can easily dehydrate and experience side effects.

2. Supplement your diet with sodium, potassium, and magnesium.
To get enough potassium, add avocados and leafy greens such as spinach to your diet.Add a little salt to each meal and to water to replenish sodium levels. Magnesium is another important mineral that can significantly ease your transition to ketosis. It is important to help you prevent and eliminate cramps, improve sleep quality and increase insulin sensitivity. Simply add pumpkin seeds, almonds, and spinach to your diet.

3. Do exercises with low intensity.

When you wake up, fill the bottle with water and a pinch of salt, and go for a walk. The walk should be at a pace where you can easily talk without gasping.It is desirable to walk for about an hour. As you continue walking, you should feel better and better and more and more awake. This is a form of low-intensity exercise that will help increase fat burning, and you will not have to suffer from keto flu.

4. Good sleep is the key to success.

Another way to reduce stress levels is to ensure good sleep. Good sleep is especially important for
ketogenic diets.

<u>HOW TO KNOW WHEN YOU ARE IN KETOSIS?</u>

There are some key signs of ketosis by which you can determine that your body is in this state.

The following symptoms are indicative of ketosis:

- Dry mouth
- Bad or "fruity" breath, metallic taste in the mouth
- Strong urine odor
- Poor appetite.
- Euphoric feeling, excess energy
- Increased thirst
- Headache
- Tiredness

<u>GETTING INTO KETOSIS. EASY STEPS</u>

Entering the state of ketosis is quite simple, but at first glance, it may seem complicated and confusing.
Here is what you need to do in order of importance:

1. Limit your carbohydrates.

Most people tend to focus only on pure carbohydrates. If you need great results, limit them. Try to stay below 20 grams of pure carbohydrates and below 35grams of carbohydrates per day.

2. Limit protein intake.

Too much protein can lead to lower levels of ketosis. Ideal for weight loss between 0.6 g and 0.8 g protein per pound of lean body mass.

3. Stop worrying about fat.

During the ketogenic diet, fat is the main source of energy - so make sure you feed your body enough. Being on a keto diet, you do not lose weight because of hunger.

4. Drink water.

Try to drink about 1 gallon (3.8 liters) of water per day. It helps not only to regulate many vital body functions but also to control hunger levels.

5. Stop snacking.

Weight loss tends to improve when you have fewer insulin splashes during the day. Unnecessary snacks can stop or slow down weight loss.

6. Start fasting.

This can be a great tool for raising ketones throughout the day.

7. Add exercise.

It is known that exercise is improving. If you want to make the most of your ketogenic diet, consider adding 20-30 minutes of exercise per day. Even a short walk can help regulate weight loss and blood sugar levels.

Note: Always be vigilant and make sure that you check the composition of the product on the labels. You will often find hidden carbohydrates in foods that seem useful during keto.

<u>FOODS TO AVOID</u>

Any food that is high in carbs should be eliminated.

Here is a list of foods that need to be eliminated on a ketogenic diet:

- **Sugary foods:**Soda which means carbonated soft drinks or minerals, fruit juice, smoothies, cake, ice cream, candy, etc.

- **Grains or starches:**Wheat-based products, rice, pasta, cereal, noodles, yam, cassava, semovita, corn etc.

- **Fruit:**All fruit, except small portions of berries like strawberries.

- **Beans or legumes:**Peas, kidney beans, lentils, chickpeas, etc.

- **Root vegetables and tubers:**Potatoes, sweet potatoes, carrots, parsnips, etc.

- **Low-fat or dairy products:** These are highly processed and often high in carbs.

- **Some condiments or sauces:** These often contain sugar and unhealthy fat.

- **Unhealthy fats:** Limit your intake of processed vegetable oils, mayonnaise, etc.

- **Alcohol:** Due to their carb content, many alcoholic beverages can throw you out of ketosis.

- **Sugar-free diet foods:** These are often high in sugar alcohols, which can affect ketone levels in some cases. These foods also tend to be highly processed.

<u>FOODS TO EAT</u>

Base the majority of your meals around these foods:

- **Meat:** Red meat, steak, ham, sausage, bacon, chicken and turkey. Yes I know you are surprised about red meat and all you have heard about it, but trust me; it is very required in this diet. Do not forget that this diet is based on eating healthy fats, which helps you burn weight faster than you think and all the aforementioned meat are all healthy.

- **Fatty fish:** Such as salmon, trout, tuna and mackerel.

- **Eggs:** Look for pastured or omega-3 whole eggs.

- **Butter and cream:** Look for grass-fed when possible.

- **Cheese:** Unprocessed cheese (cheddar, goat, cream, blue or mozzarella).

- **Nuts and seeds:** Almonds, walnuts, flax seeds, pumpkin seeds, chia seeds, etc.

- **Healthy oils:** Primarily extra virgin olive oil, coconut oil and avocado oil.

- **Avocados:** Whole avocados or freshly made guacamole.

- **Low-carb veggies:** Most green veggies, tomatoes, onions, peppers, etc.

- **Condiments:** You can use salt, pepper and various healthy herbs and spices.

<u>SHOPPING LIST</u>

Oils and refills
Olive oil:- for salads and frying, and baking

Almond oil
Good oil for soups, fruit puree and baking

Hazelnut oil
Add the taste of "Nutella" to the desserts, but without sugar.

Soymilk

Peanut butter.
A good combination for, soups (for example, peanut), dough for biscuits and keto bread.

Natural sweeteners
100% maple syrup Monk, Stevia etc. At the same time it is important to understand that it is still sugar and use it carefully.

Gluten free Flour

Flours with no gluten like almond, coconut soy etc are great choice for the ketogenic diet. Almond flour is ideal for cookies, crumbs, and pies.

Vanilla extract

It gives a wonderful taste to cakes, desserts, ice cream. It is important to buy an extract with natural vanilla, and not an artificial flavoring.

Apple cider vinegar

Together with baking soda, it perfectly loosens the dough for muffins and pies.

Coconut oil (solid and liquid)

Unlike a liquid, it does not give the dishes a coconut flavor, so you can safely use in any recipe with butter.

Curry paste

Add spicy to vegetable stews and curry.

Nutritional Yeast

They improve the taste of cheeses, curry, risotto, vegetable dishes, and savory pies and crumbs.

<u>PRODUCTS TO EAT ON KETO DIET</u>

White cabbage
Broccoli
Cauliflower
Cashew
Brussels sprouts
Chinese cabbage (salad)
Green lettuce leaves
Celery Stalks
Onion
Green beans
Zucchini
Cucumbers
Tomatoes (very few)
Greenery
Mushrooms
Meat
Bird
Fish
Seafood
Offal
Eggs
Cheese
Cottage cheese
Butter
Vegetable oils

<u>PROHIBITED PRODUCTS ON KETO DIET</u>

Sugar and Honey
Candy, chocolate, ice cream
Desserts
Pastries
Cookies
Waffles
Preserves, jams
Dried fruits
Cereals
Bread
Pasta
Fruits
Powdered drinks
Crab sticks and meat (imitation)
Soda
Sweet dairy products
Starch
Potatoes, beets and other starchy vegetables
Beer
Products on fructose and sorbitol
Milk
Juices
Nuts

Bran
Legumes and a whole lot of others not
mentioned.

KETOGENIC SMOOTHIES

LEMON BERRIES SMOOTHIE

Ingredients
- 1/2 cup of broccoli
- 1 cup blueberries
- ½ cup lemon juice
- 1 cup strawberries
- 1 cup water

Directions:

- Add all the ingredients into the blender and ice cubes as required.

- Blend till you get the desired consistency. Pour into a glass and drink away.

- Pour and drink.

SPINACH AND PUMPKIN SMOOTHIE

Ingredients:

1 peeled lemon
1/2 peeled pumpkin
1 cup spinach
1/2 cup water
1 tablespoon flaxseed
Ice cubes

Directions:

- Add all the ingredients into the blender and ice cubes as required.

- Blend till you get the desired consistency. Pour into a glass and drink away.

BROCCOLI AND SPINACH SMOOTHIE

Ingredients:-

- ½ cup broccoli
- 1 cup spinach
- ½ cup cabbage
- 1 cup apple Cider Vinegar
- 1/2 cup water

Directions:

- Add all the ingredients into the blender and ice cubes as required.

- Blend till you get the desired consistency. Pour into a glass and drink away.

STRAWBERRY AVOCADO SMOOTHIE

Ingredients:

- 1/2 cup Strawberry chunks
- 1/2 avocado, diced
- 1 cup (2 handfuls) fresh spinach
- 1/2 cup coconut water
- 1 tablespoon hemp seeds

Directions:
- Add all the ingredients into the blender and ice cubes as required.

- Blend till you get the desired consistency. Pour into a glass and drink away.

DETOX SMOOTHIE

Ingredients:

- 1 cup organic kale
- 1/2 cup parsley
- 1 cup cucumber
- 1/2 cup pineapple
- 1 lemon
- 1/2 avocado
- 1 cup unsweetened green tea
- 1 tablespoon fresh grated ginger

Directions:

- Squeeze the juice from the lemon into the blender.

- Add the rest of the ingredients and blend to desired consistency.

- Pour and drink.

ROMAN LETTUCE SMOOTHIE

Ingredients

- 1 cup water
- 1 cup organic, chopped romaine lettuce
- 1/2 cup spinach
- 1/2 cup chopped celery

Directions:

- Add all the ingredients into the blender and ice cubes as required.

- Blend till you get the desired consistency.

- Pour and drink.

KALE AND GINGER SMOOTHIE

Ingredients:

- 2 large kale leaves
- 1/2 bunch of parsley
- 1/2 cup cucumber
- 1/2 apple
- 1 cup celery
- 1/2 cup water
- 1 tablespoons grated ginger

Directions:

- Add all the ingredients into the blender and ice cubes as required.

- Blend till you get the desired consistency.

- Pour and drink.

STRAWBERRY AND SPINACH SMOOTHIE

Ingredients:

- 1 cup spinach
- 1 cup strawberries
- 1 cup cucumber
- 1 tablespoon hemp seeds (optional)
- 1 cup water

Directions:

- Add all the ingredients into the blender and ice cubes as required.

- Blend till you get the desired consistency.

- Pour and drink.

TROPICAL SMOOTHIE DREAM

Ingredients:
- 1/2 cup parsley
- 1/2 cup cucumber
- 1 Cucumber
- 1 stalks celery
- 1/2 tablespoon grated ginger
- 1 cup coconut water

Directions:

- Add all the ingredients into the blender and ice cubes as required.

- Blend till you get the desired consistency.

- Pour and drink.

BEETROOT AND AVOCADO SMOOTHIE

Ingredients:
1 Avocado
1 Celery stalk
4 oz Strawberry
Lemon juice to taste

Directions:

- Add all the ingredients into the blender and ice cubes as required.

- Blend till you get the desired consistency.

- Pour and drink.

MIGHTY BERRY SMOOTHIE

Ingredients

1 cup blackberries
1 cup strawberries
4 oz Frozen raspberries
10 Hazelnuts

Directions:

- Add all the ingredients into the blender and ice cubes as required.

- Blend till you get the desired consistency.

- Beat the nuts in a blender (so that small crumb remains).

- Pour the smoothie into a glass, sprinkle with nuts and drink

CHIA BERRIES SMOOTHIE

Ingredients

7 fl. oz Yoghurt
2 cup Blueberry
1 tablespoon Goji berry
1 tablespoon Chia seed

Directions:

- Add all the ingredients into the blender and ice cubes as required.

- Blend till you get the desired consistency.

- Pour and drink.

ALMOND SMOOTHIE

Ingredients

17 fl. oz. Almond milk
2 tablespoons Almond oil
2 Avocados
1 tablespoon Cinnamon

Directions:

- Add all the ingredients into the blender and ice cubes as required.

- Blend till you get the desired consistency.

- Pour and drink.

<u>MINTY AVOCADO SMOOTHIE</u>

Ingredients

4 oz Strawberry
A handful of Mint
1 tiny baby carrot
1 Avocado

Directions:

- Add all the ingredients into the blender and ice cubes as required.

- Blend till you get the desired consistency.

- Pour into a glass and drink away.

NUTTY AND CHOCOLATE SMOOTHIES

Ingredients

1 tablespoon Nutella
2 oz Walnuts
Coconut flakes
1 cup Coconut milk

Directions:

- Add all the ingredients into the blender and ice cubes as required.

- Blend till you get the desired consistency.

- Pour into a glass and drink away.

SPICY TOMATO SMOOTHIE WITH PUMPKIN SEEDS

Ingredients

2 oz Celery stalk
1 Beetroot
1 baby Carrots
2 Tomatoes
2 Garlic, cloves
¼ teaspoon Curry
¼ teaspoon Turmeric
¼ teaspoon Cumin
2 oz Peeled pumpkin seeds

Directions

- Pure all in a blender, pre-cut the ingredients into cubes.

- Instead of tomatoes, you can use tomato juice.

GREEN POWER SMOOTHIE

Ingredients:

Spinach

Matcha powder

Unsweetened almond milk

Heavy cream

Celery,

Strawberries

Stevia

Directions:

- In a blender, combine washed spinach, matcha powder, unsweetened almond milk, heavy cream, celery, strawberries and stevia to sweeten.
- Then blend all together and enjoy.

KETOGENIC FAT BOMBS

<u>FAT BOMBS</u>

Ingredients

½ cup Butter
½ cup Coconut oil
½ cup Sour cream
½ cup Cream cheese
2 tablespoon Erythritol
25 drops Liquid stevia
2 teaspoons Cocoa powder
1 teaspoon Vanilla extract
2 medium strawberries

Directions

- Using a blender, mix all the ingredients (except cocoa powder, vanilla, and strawberry) in a bowl.
- Divide the mixture between 3 bowls and add cocoa powder to one, vanilla to another, and strawberries to third.
- Pour the chocolate mixture into the mold and place in the freezer for 30minutes.

- Repeat the process with vanilla and strawberry layers. Now put all freeze for at least 1 hour.

COCONUT AND ALMONDS FAT BOMBS

Ingredients

1 cup Coconut chips
3 tablespoon Fat coconut milk
3 tablespoon Coconut oil (melted)
½ teaspoon Vanilla extract
4 oz Chocolate chips with no sugar
A pinch of salt
2 oz Keto-friendly sweetener
24 Almond, pieces

Directions

- Put 2 tablespoons of melted coconut oil, coconut milk, sweetener, coconut chips, vanilla extract and salt in a small bowl.

- Divide the mixture into 12 servings and place them on a baking sheet with parchment paper.

- Put in the freezer for 5 minutes, and then put on each fat bomb 1-2 pieces of almonds.

- Melt the chocolate chips together with 2 teaspoons of coconut oil in the microwave.

- Remove the bombs from the freezer, pour each of the chocolate mixture and cool.

SPICY FAT BOMBS

Ingredients

6 MCT powder, scoops
10 Liquid stevia, drops
1 tablespoon Turmeric
1 tablespoon Black sesame seeds
A pinch of black pepper
½ tsp Cinnamon
2½ fl. oz Warm water

Directions

- Mix all the dry ingredients in a small bowl.

- Add warm water and mix until smooth.

- Spread the mixture evenly over 12 silicone molds.

- Put in the fridge so that the fat bombs are well frozen.

- Always keep them frozen; otherwise, they will quickly melt.

COFFEE FAT BOMBS

Ingredients

4 oz Butter
2 oz Ghee butter (melted)
2 oz Heavy cream
1 tablespoon Milk to your taste
Double espresso
2 oz Keto sweetener of choice
1 teaspoon Vanilla extract
A pinch of salt

Directions

- Add all ingredients to a small food processor and whip at high speed until airy.

- Add sweetener to taste

- Pour into molds and refrigerate for 30 minutes

ALMOND COCOA FAT BOMBS

Ingredients

1 cup Almond oil
1 cup Coconut oil
2 tablespoon Cocoa powder
2 tablespoon Erythritol, to your taste

Directions

- Mix almond and coconut oil in a microwave dish.

- Heat the mixture in the microwave for 30-45 seconds and mix until a homogeneous mass.

- Add erythritol and cocoa powder, and mix to complete the mix.

- Pour the mass into mini cupcake molds and refrigerate in the refrigerator.

PUMPKIN FAT SPICE BOMBS

Ingredients

8 oz cashews
4 oz macadamia nuts
4 oz Coconut chips
3 fl. oz Pumpkin puree
2 tablespoon MCT oils
2 teaspoon Cinnamon, ground
2 teaspoon Ginger, ground
Avocado oil

Directions

- Put all the ingredients in a food processor and mix to form dough.

- Lightly grease your hands with avocado oil.

- Using a spoon, take about 5 -4 oz. of the batter into lightly oiled hands and form a ball and repeat the process

- Decorate fat bombs with savory coconut chips. Such fatty bombs can be eaten immediately, or stored in are refrigerator/freezer.

CHEESE FAT BOMBS IN BACON

Ingredients

8 oz Mozzarella cheese
4 tablespoon Almond flour
4 tablespoon tbsp Butter, melted
3 tablespoon tbsp Psyllium powder
1 Egg
Salt, to taste
1 tablespoon Black pepper
1/8 tablespoon Garlic powder
1/8 tablespoon tsp Onion powder
20 Bacon, slices
1 cup oil or lard (for frying)

Directions

- Microwave half the cheese for 45-60 seconds or until it melts and becomes sticky.

- Heat the butter in the microwave for 15-20 seconds until completely melted, and then mix it with cheese and egg.

- Add psyllium husks, almond flour, and spices. Mix again and lay out the dough in a rectangle.

- Fill the rectangle with the rest of the cheese and fold it in half (horizontally), then in half (vertically).

- Trim the edges and form into a rectangle.

- Cut 20 square pieces. Wrap each piece of dough with a piece of bacon, using toothpicks to fasten it.

- Put each piece in boiling oil and cook for 1-3 minutes.

KETOGENIC SAUCES

<u>KETO HOMEMADE MAYO</u>

Ingredients

6 fl. oz Olive oil
4 fl. oz Coconut oil
1 Egg
2 Egg yolks
1 tablespoon Dijon mustard
Pinch of salt and smoked paprika
3 drops Liquid stevia

Directions

- Start by adding oils to the blender bowl to measure them. Make sure your coconut oil is not hot.

- Add all other ingredients.

- Start mixing without lifting the blender.

- Continue mixing by holding the blender at the bottom of the container.

- Move the blender up and down until the mayonnaise is fully emulsified.

- Put mayonnaise in a glass jar with a lid and place in the refrigerator. If you are using whey, leave on a rack for 7 hours, then refrigerate.

NOTE:
If you do not have a dip blender, put all ingredients, except butter, in your blender or food processor, and turn it on. Very carefully and very slowly start adding oil. As the mayonnaise begins to emulsify, you can start adding oil a little faster, until you reach a steady stream.

HOMEMADE SAUCE

Ingredients

1 Onion
2 tablespoon Chili peppers, dried
3 tablespoon No-sugar ketchup
2 tablespoon Coconut oil
Salt, to taste

Directions

- Cut the onion and mix until smooth. Set aside.

- Cut the dried chilies and remove the seeds. Boil the peppers for about 30minutes or until soft. Then turn the pepper into a paste.

- In a heated frying pan, melt coconut oil. Then add all the ingredients and mix thoroughly.

KETO KETCHUP LOW CARB

Ingredients

3/4 cup Tomato paste
2 tablespoon Apple cider vinegar
2 tablespoon Keto sweetener
Pinch of salt
1 tablespoon Garlic powder
3/4 tablespoon Onion powder
Pinch of Cayenne Pepper
1 cup Water

Directions

- Add all the ingredients into a large bowl and whisk well.

- Adjust the salt and sweetener to taste.

<u>KETO SAUCE</u>

Ingredients

6 Egg yolks
1 drop Worcestershire sauce
1 drop Low carb hot sauce
1 Lemon, juice
Pinch of salt
Ground black pepper
8 oz Butter

Directions

- Put the ingredients in a blender with the exception of the pepper and butter

- Heat the butter in the microwave for 2-3 minutes

- Set the blender to low speed and quickly pour the oil through the top of the blender.

- Beat about 10-15 seconds until smooth.

TAPENADE SAUCE

Ingredients

1 cup Black olives in brine
1 oz Capers
4 fl. oz Mix Olive and Avocado oils
2 Garlic, cloves
3 tablespoon Lemon juice
2 tablespoon Apple cider vinegar
1 cup Fresh basil
1 cup Fresh parsley
½ tablespoon Black pepper

Directions

- Put all the ingredients in a blender or food processor, and beat at low speed until completely homogeneous.

- Pour into dishes and store in the refrigerator for up to 1 week.

<u>MEAT SAUCE</u>

Ingredients

1 Shallot
4 Garlic, cloves
½ cup Cilantro
½ cup Parsley
1 Lemon juice
3 tablespoon Red wine vinegar
2 tablespoon tsp Crushed red pepper
Pinch of salt and black pepper
¼ cup Olive oil

Directions

- Mix all ingredients except olive oil in a food processor. Continuing to beat, pour the oil through the top of a continuous stream.

- Season to taste and add more oil or a couple of tablespoons of water, if necessary, so that the sauce is more fluid.

<u>KETO TOFU</u>

Ingredients

1 lb. Soft tofu
1 tablespoon Olive oil
5 tablespoon tsp Lemon juice
2 tablespoon Apple vinegar
1 tablespoon keto sweetener
Salt, to taste

Directions

- Put all the ingredients in a blender.

- Beat five minutes until the mass is very creamy and smooth.

- Cool the vegetarian sour cream for two hours so that it can thicken.

- Serve with what you want

CAESAR SAUCE

Ingredients

2 ½ oz Mayonnaise
2 tablespoon Lemon juice
2 Shredded Anchovies
2 Worcestershire sauce
2 Dijon mustard
3 Garlic cloves
Salt and ground black pepper

Directions

- Crush the three heads of garlic in a bowl.

- Add to the garlic anchovies, Worcester sauce, lemon juice, Dijon mustard and mix.

- Pour the mayonnaise into the bowl and mix thoroughly until smooth.

- Serve as a Caesar salad dressing and do not forget to sprinkle Parmesan on top.

CILANTRO PESTO

Ingredients

2 oz Cilantro
2 oz Parsley
1 tablespoon Olive oil
9 Almond, nut (pre-soaked and peeled)
2 tablespoon tbsp Pine nut
1 tablespoon Olive oil
Salt, to taste

Directions

- Rinse the cilantro and parsley, dip it in boiling water for a few seconds cool

- Add the nuts and grind in a blender

- Add oil and salt and stir for a few more seconds.

<u>VEGETABLE GUACAMOLE</u>

Ingredients

1 tablespoon Red onion, crushed
1 Lime (juice)
2 Avocados
1 Tomato
Celery
2 Fresh chopped chili peppers,
Salt, to taste

Directions

- Cut the avocado in half, remove stone and scrub the pulp with a spoon.

- Combine with the remaining ingredients. And blend all until smooth.

KETOGENIC ICECREAM

<u>AVOCADO, COCONUT AND CUCUMBER YOGHURT.</u>

A little lemon juice

1 Avocado

1 cucumber

Shredded coconut

Coconut milk

1 full spoon of mayonnaise and

Complaint sweetener

Direction:

- In a blender add Avocado, Cucumber, and shredded Coconut, a full spoon of mayonnaise, coconut milk and complaint sweetener of choice.
- Then blend together add a squeezed of lemon as you blend.
- Put in the fridge to be taken chilled.

<u>KETO ICE CREAM</u>

Ingredients:

Greek Yoghurt (Full fat and Unsweetened)

Eggs

Cocoa Powder (unsweetened)

Stevia

Method:

- Put all in a blender and blend till well incorporated.
- Use a mixer as well. I used a mixer.
- Pour into a bowl and freezer for 4-6hours.
- Serve immediately.

<u>AVOCADO CUSTARD</u>

Ingredients:

Avocado

Mayonnaise

Butter

Coconut milk

Stevia

Method:

- Blend your avocado pear,
- Add little mayonnaise, butter, coconut milk, and stevia to sweeten it and blend again.
- Pour in a container and freeze.
- Serve when chilled.

KETOGENIC SWALLOW

<u>RUTABAGA SWALLOW</u>

Ingredients:

Water

Psyllium husk or any other keto binder

Rutabaga

Directions:

- Cut the rutabaga
- Boil until tender,
- Pour in blender and blend till smooth,
- Pour back in pot, add little psyllium husk to bind and mix.
- Remove from heat and wrap in a cling film and serve with soup of choice.

COCONUT SWALLOW

Ingredients:

Coconut flour

Water

Psyllium husk or any other keto binder

Directions:

- Put a pan with water on heat.
- Bring water to boil, add half cup coconut flour, and stir.
- Add a tablespoon of husk.
- Continue stirring till very firm, remove from heat and wrap in a cling film
- Serve with soup of choice.

CABBAGE SWALLOW

Ingredients:

Cabbage

Water

Psyllium husk or any other keto binder

Directions:

- Slice the cabbage into smaller pieces
- Blend until smooth
- Sieve water out from blended cabbage
- Add little water in a pot
- Add the blended cabbage into the boiling water and stir.
- Add a teaspoon of psyllium husk
- Once it thickens, scoop and wrap in a cling film.
- Serve with any soup of choice

EGG PLANT SWALLOW

Ingredients:

Egg plant

Water

Psyllium husk

Directions:

- Cut the egg plant
- Blend with little water
- Squeeze with a cheese cloth to help drain out most of its water
- Put on heat and add the psyllium husk until it sticks together
- Scoop and wrap in a cling film
- Serve with any soup of choice

<u>CAULIFLOWER SWALLOW</u>

Ingredients:

Cauliflower

Water

Psyllium husk

Directions:

- Cut into sizable pieces per boil for a minute or less depending on the heat.
- Blend, drain out the water
- Put on a low heat and add psyllium husk as binding agent
- When thicken scoop and wrap in a cling fling and let to cool
- Serve with any soup of choice

COCONUT SWALLOW

Ingredients:

Coconut flour

Water

Psyllium husk

DIRECTION:

- Bring a water to boil
- Add half cup coconut flour and stir.
- Add a 1 tablespoon of husk, and when it thickens, remove from heat
- Scoop and wrap in a cling film and let to cool
- Serve with any soup of choice.

<u>GARDEN EGG SWALLOW</u>

Ingredients:

Garden Egg

Water

Psyllium husk

Directions:

- Cut garden egg
- Blend with little water
- Squeeze with a cheese cloth to help drain out most of its water
- Put on heat and add the psyllium husk until it sticks together
- Scoop and wrap in a cling film
- Serve with any soup of choice

<u>PUMPKIN SWALLOW</u>

Ingredients:

Pumpkin

Water

Psyllium husk

Directions:

- Cut pumpkin
- Boil and blend with little water
- Put back on heat and add the psyllium husk until it sticks together
- Scoop and wrap in a cling film
- Serve with any soup of choice

CUCUMBER SWALLOW

Ingredients:

Cucumber

Water

Psyllium husk

Directions:

- Cut cucumber
- Blend with little water
- Squeeze with a cheese cloth to help drain out most of its water
- Put on heat and add the psyllium husk until it sticks together
- Scoop and wrap in a cling film
- Serve with any soup of choice

KETOGENIC AFRICAN SOUPS

ASSORTED MEAT PEPPER SOUP

Ingredients

700g Assorted Meats aka Offal

Onion

5 Scotch Bonnet thinly chopped

3 Cloves Garlic

2 Tablespoons Pepper Soup Spice

1 grated Ginger Root

1 Teaspoon Cayenne Pepper

3 Tablespoons Dry or fresh Basil leaves

1 Tablespoon Black Pepper

Bouillon cubes

Salt to taste

DIRECTIONS:

- Wash your meats thoroughly and transfer into a pot.

- Add blended Chopped Garlic, Onions and Ginger. Also add the bouillon cubes and salt to taste.

- Boil the Offal which comprises of either cow or goat intestines Kidney, Liver, and Heart separately. Boil without any water.

- Place on medium heat and allow the meats boil for 30 minutes to absorb the spices and onions thereby producing its own liquid.

- Then add enough water to cover the meat and cook till soft.

- When the meats are soft, add the Chopped or blended peppers combine and cook for 10 minutes.

- Add the Pepper soup Spice. Taste for seasoning and adjust if necessary.

- Add the chopped Basil leaves, then, down from heat

- Your Soup is ready.

OKRO PEPPER SOUP

Ingredients

Shrimp

Catfish cut into chunks

Stockfish

Smoked fish or any smoked fish

Okra chopped or finely sliced

Pumpkin leaves (Ugwu) or Spinach sliced

Onion large chopped finely

Scotch bonnet

3 tbsp crayfish ground

Cups water

2 bouillon cubes

Cayenne pepper

Salt to taste

1/2 Cup Periwinkle

DIRECTIONS:

- Chop the okra into tiny bits.

- Add water to a pot and boil the washed stockfish without ingredients until soft.

- Remove stockfish from the pot leaving only the water.

- Into the water add onion, scotch bonnet, salt, seasoning cubes, and ground pepper in a pot and leave to boil

- Place the clean, fresh fish in the seasoned water and cook on medium heat for few minutes.

- Add the pepper soup spice and Crayfish and continue to cook for a couple of more minutes until the fish is well-cooked.

- Remove fish from the sauce and set aside

- Add shrimps and periwinkle and cook till shrimps.

- Add the okra and cook for about two minutes.

- Stir in the sliced vegetables and return the fish back to the pot of soup. Leave to simmer for 5 minutes

- Taste and adjust seasoning as desired.

NIGERIAN GOAT MEAT PEPPER SOUP

Ingredients:

Basil or Uziza leaves

Goat meat

3 Tablespoons Crayfish

1 Tablespoons Pepper soup spice

Red Chili flakes

1 Tablespoon blended Garlic

1 Tablespoon blended Ginger

 Salt to taste

1tablespoon blended Onion

4 Scotch bonnet

1 Bouillon cube

4 Cups Water

Directions:

- Cut the Goat meat into cutlets and wash thoroughly.

- Transfer the meat into the Pot, add salt, bouillon cube, peppers, ginger, garlic and Onion and cook for 30 minutes.

- Add the pepper soup spice, red chili flakes and crayfish. Leave it to cook for another 10 minutes.

- Add in the basil or uziza leaves and let it simmer for another 5 minutes.

- Serve hot.

<u>KALE (EFO RIRO) SOUP</u>

Ingredients:

400g Kale Leaves, Washed and Chopped

4 Red African Bell Peppers

2-3 Scotch bonnet

1/2 Cup Palm oil

1 Cup Meat or Chicken Stock

2 Medium Size Red Onions

1kg Boiled Assorted Meats aka Offal

Smoked Stockfish, Shredded

Smoked Cat fish, Shredded

3 Tablespoons Locust beans (Iru)

1/2 Cup Smoked Prawns

2 bouillon Cubes

3 Tablespoons Ground Crayfish

Salt to taste

Direction:

- Blend the Scotch bonnets, African Bell peppers and Onion coarsely and set aside then chop the second Onion and set aside.

- Place a medium size pot on medium heat. Add the Palm oil, leave to heat up for 3 minutes and add the Chopped onions, fry till translucent.

- Add the Locust Beans, fry to release the flavor, add half of the Crayfish, fry for a minute.

- Add the blended Pepper, bouillon cubes and Salt to taste, leave to boil for 15-20 minutes until the pepper dries out and the size reduces by almost half.

- The pepper at this time should be in a thick consistency and the oil should have settled on the top.

- If the consistency is too thick, add a bit of the meat stock/ chicken stock, if you haven't got stock, just add water, and be careful not to add too much.

- If you added Stock, allow to boil for 2-3 minutes to combine, and then add the assorted meats, stir and combine. Leave to cook for 10 minutes.

- Then add the Prawns, the rest of the Crayfish, shredded Stockfish and Smoked Catfish

- Combine and taste, adjust seasoning if required. Leave to cook for 4minutes

- Add the Chopped Kale leaves, combine thoroughly. Leave to cook for 3 minutes

- Switch off the heat leave to

simmer with the residual heat for 2 minutes.

- Your Kale Efo Riro is ready

OGBONO SOUP

Ingredients

1 Cup blended Ogbono or wild mango seed

4 Cups stock Beef or Chicken

Meat Tripe, cow skin or Fish of choice

1 Cup Stock Fish

Salt to taste

2 bouillon cubes

1/2 Tablespoon Cayenne pepper

1 Tbsp Crayfish ground

Pumpkin leaves, Kale or spinach Greens

1 Cup Periwinkle

1/3 Cup Palm Oil

Directions:

- Cut the beef wash, put into a pot and season with Salt, bullion

powder (or stock cubes).
- Add the diced Onions and the cayenne pepper.
- Allow to boil for about 20 to 30 minutes depending on how tender you want the meat to be.
- Once the meat is almost done, add the stockfish and cook for 5 minutes or till soft.
- Blend the Ogbono seeds and add it to the boiling meat: Be sure you have enough stock in the pot.
- Stir well until the Ogbono is well dissolved in the stock
- Stir in the periwinkles, crayfish, and Palm Oil and leave to cook for another 5 minutes.
- Now turn down the heat then add your leafy greens. Leave to simmer for another 2 to 3 minutes.
- Serve with your favorite swallow and ENJOY!

<u>OKRO SOUP</u>

Ingredients:

2 cups Okra half minced and half sliced

1 red bell pepper

Smoked Turkey wings

1 Small onion minced

1 habanero pepper

3 Tbsp crayfish

1/2 lb Spinach

1 lb shrimps

1 Dry Fish large

4 Tbsp Locust bean

Palm oil

1 Tsp Seasoning powder

4 small cups water

Direction:

- Boil the Smoked Turkey wings with salt, seasoning powder and minced Onions. Cook till tender.

- While the meat is boiling, mince half of the onions in a food processor or a chopper and slice the other half. Set aside

- Mince the red bell pepper and habanero pepper in the chopper and set aside

- When the meat becomes tender, add the minced pepper, crayfish, and locust bean and leave to cook for about 10 minutes.

- Shred and add the washed dry fish and leave to soften for about five minutes.

- Add the palm oil, shrimps and the minced and sliced okro. Leave to cook for about 3 to 5 minutes.

- Stir in the spinach and mix until wilted.

- Remove from heat immediately and serve.

<u>CHICKEN STIR FRY WITH SPINACH</u>

Ingredients:

2kg Boneless Chicken Thigh Cut into little pieces

1kg Baby Spinach

1 Onion Diced

1 Cup Tomato Sauce

1 teaspoon Salt

1 Tablespoon Oil

Directions:

- Heat the Oil in a Pan, over high heat until shimmering.

- Add the Onions and Saute until it's translucent

- Add the Chicken, season with Salt and black pepper and stir-fry until it's browned

- Pour in the Tomato sauce and cook

for another 5 minutes

- Add the Spinach in handfuls and cook until it's wilted - about 1 or 2 minutes

- Remove from heat immediately.

- Serve and Enjoy!

EGUSI (MELON) SOUP WITH OKAZI

Ingredients:

Assorted meats also known as Offal

1 Cup Ground Egusi

1 small Cup Palm Oil

2 Cups Chicken/ Meat Stock

3 African Red Bell Pepper

2 Medium Onions

2 Scotch Bonnet

1 Cup Thinly Chopped Ukazi leaves

3 Heaped Tablespoons Ground Crayfish

1/4 cup Smoked Prawns

1 Medium Size Smoked Fish or Stockfish

1/2 Cup raw Prawns (Optional)

2 Bouillon cubes to taste

Salt to taste

Direction:

- Blend the bell peppers, Scotch bonnet and 1 Onion roughly and set aside.

- Soak the thinly sliced Okazi leaves in hot water for 5 minutes, rinse to remove all traces of dirt.

- Transfer the Egusi into a frying pan and place on medium heat. Toast for 3-5 minutes; shaking the pan vigorously when it begins to toast then blend the Egusi with onions and set aside.

- Boil the meats with onions and bouillon cubes.

- When the meats are almost soft, add the stock fish and cook till soft.

- Place a pot on medium heat, add the palm oil, when it's hot, chop half of an onion and add into it.

- Sauté the onions till translucent, then add the locust beans, sauté for 2 minutes

- Then add half of the crayfish, continue to sauté for a minute.

- Add the blended Pepper and bouillon cubes. Do not add Salt.

- Fry the Pepper for 10 minutes, at this time the size should have reduced by almost half and oil should have settled on the top.

- Now add 1 cup of stock or water and continue to cook, be careful not to add too much stock or water.

- Let this fry for a further 5 minutes, then add the blended Egusi, then add the boiled meats and smoked fish.

- Allow this to cook for 5 minutes, and then add the shredded smoked fish and prawns.

- Now add the soaked Okazi leaves, stir and combine, taste for salt and seasoning, adjust if necessary. Cook for 8 minutes or until the leaves become soft. Okazi is a tough vegetable and as such, will need a while to soften.

- Turn off the heat off and let it simmer with the residual heat for 2-3 minutes.

LUMPY EGUSI (MELON)STEW

Ingredients

2 Cups Melon Ground (Egusi)

1/2 Cup Water

1/2 Cup Palm Oil

2 Tablespoons Crayfish

1 Cup Meat Stock

2 Bouillon Cubes

Salt to taste

1 Pound Vegetables (Chopped)

1/2 Pound Smoked Fish shredded into chunky pieces

2 Medium Sized Onions

Beef Chicken, Fish etc

DIRECTIONS:

- Pour the Egusi (Melon) and one diced Onion in a bowl and use your hands to massage the Onions with the Egusi. This will infuse some onion flavor into the Egusi and the Oil in the Egusi will also be activated.

- Add Water and mix together to form a paste and set aside

- Add some Oil in a Pan, enough to deep fry the Egusi and fry for about 5 minutes turning halfway through on a medium heat (don't over fry this else you'll get a crunchy melon) - You will literally see the Egusi curdle up straightaway

- Remove from heat and drain the Oil (You don't need all that Oil) and set aside

- Add a little Palm Oil in another Pan (I used part of the Oil I drained from the Egusi) and add the second Onion (diced) and let that cook for a couple of seconds then add the Sauce and also allow that to cook for 5 minutes.

- Add the Crayfish, Salt to taste, Stock cubes, Smoked Fish (you can add that later if you don't want the Fish broken into pieces) and Stock.

- Now add the fried Egusi to the sauce and allow it to cook for 20 minutes on a low to medium heat - check this constantly to avoid burning and add Water or stock if it's getting too dry.

- Finally, add the Spinach or choice of Vegetables with Meat or Fish and leave it to simmer for 5 minutes more or less depending on how tough or soft the vegetable is.

- Serve and Enjoy.

<u>EDIKAI IKONG SOUP</u>

INGREDIENTS

400g pumpkin leaves/ Ugu
200g Waterleaves
1kg boiled assorted meat
200g Periwinkle
200g boiled Dried Stock Fish
4 pieces boiled Crabs and or Snails
100g Shrimps
50g Crayfish
300ml Palm oil
1 large Onion
2 or 3 pieces red chili peppers
10g Locust beans
Bouillon cubes
Salt

METHOD:

- Fry 4 cooking spoons of palm oil into a deep cooking pan, slice in a few onions.

- Add blended pepper and allow cooking for 3 minutes. Slice in red chili peppers then steam for 3 minutes.

- Add the sliced waterleaves; do not add water because waterleaves produces water on their own. Now cook for 3 minutes.

- Add in the remaining ingredients, periwinkle, shrimps, boiled stock fish, and smoked stock fish, boiled assorted beef, crayfish, crabs, snails and locust beans.

- Season with bouillon cubes salt. Stir in all the ingredients together, and then leave for 2 minutes.

- Add the pumpkin leaves, a bit of water then stir, leave for 2 minutes.

- Serve with any keto swallow of choice.

<u>WATCH OUT</u>

Volume two of the ketogenic diary which comprises of keto cakes, keto bread and other baked products and also chicken, beef, pork and all kinds of meat preparation would be out soon.

A

KETOGENIC

3 WEEKS

MEAL PLAN

3 WEEKS WEIGHTLOSS MEAL PLAN

DAY	BREAKFAST	LUNCH	DINNER	Exercise & Water
Tuesday DAY 1 ZERO CARB	2 or 3 Eggs fried in Butter or Keto compliant Oil	Chicken or Beef cooked any way you like with 2 tablespoons Mayonnaise	Pepper soup with any Meat or Fish of your choice	Walk minimun 5,000 Steps Drink 8 glasses of water or Flat Belly Detox Drink
Wednesday DAY 2 ZERO CARB	Bacon and Sausage Or 1 can of Sardine or Tuna	Flour free Scotch eggs or 3 Boiled eggs	Any Meat or Fish Suya	Walk minimun 5,000 Steps Drink 8 glasses of water or Flat Belly Detox Drink
Thursday DAY 3 Green Veggie Day	Green veggies eg Ugwu and eggs fried in 2 tablespoons of butter	Chicken or Turkey Cooked anyway you want with GREEN Veggies	Any Meat or Fish Peppersoup	Walk minimun 5,000 Steps Drink 8 glasses of water or Flat Belly Detox Drink
Friday DAY 4 Green Veggie Day	I can of Tuna or Sardine with Cabbage or Lettuce cooked with 1 tablespoon coconut oil or butter	Green Vegetable cooked with 2 tablespoon of Keto Compliant oil and Crayfish or Shrimps	Fish Cooked anyway you want with Cucumber	Walk minimun 5,000 Steps Drink 8 glasses of water or Flat Belly Detox Drink

3 WEEKS WEIGHTLOSS MEAL PLAN

Saturday **DAY 5** **ZERO CARB**	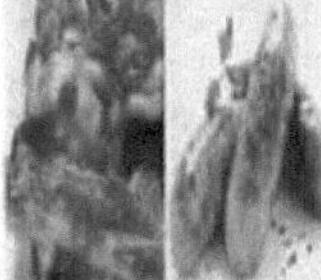 Bacon and 1 Sausage OR	 Try something new Make Asun or Isi Ewu	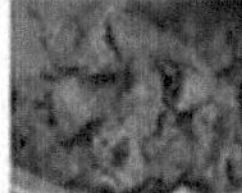 Gizzard or Snail Goatmeat cooked anyway you like	Walk minimun 7,000 Steps Drink 8 glasses of water or Flat Belly Detox Drink
Sunday **DAY 6**	 Egg Wrap Garnished with Keto Compliant ingredients	 Cauliflower or Cabbage Rice cooked any way you like with any meat	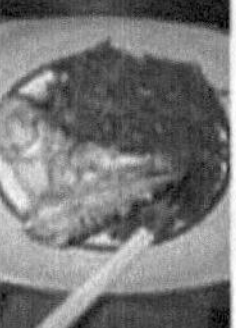 Fish or Chicken and Veggies	Drink 8 glasses of water or Flat Belly Detox Drink
Monday **DAY 7** **Zero Carb Day**	 Bullet Coffee or Tea with a can of Sardine or Tuna	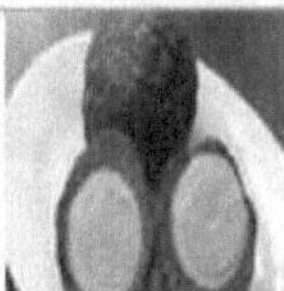 Flourless Scotch Eggs	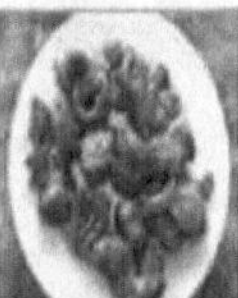 Gizzard Boiled and fried in Oil or Butter with 2 tablespoons of Mayo	Walk minimun 5,000 Steps Drink 8 glasses of water or Flat Belly Detox Drink
Tuesday **DAY 8** **ZERO CARB**			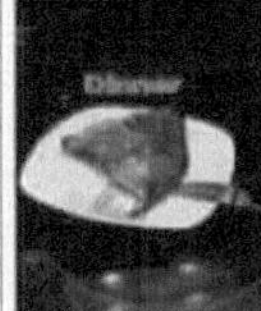	Walk minimun 5,000 Steps Drink 8 glasses of water or Flat Belly Detox

3 WEEKS WEIGHTLOSS MEAL PLAN

	2 Bacon and 2 Sausage Or 1 Can of Sardine/Tuna	Any meat pepper soup	Fried Fish and Mayo	Drink
Wednesday DAY 9 Green Veggie Day	Vegetable Salad	Any Keto Compliant Soup with Keto Compliant Swallow Or Just Soup and Meat or Fish	Chicken and Mayo Salad	Walk minimun 5,000 Steps Drink 8 glasses of water or Flat Belly Detox Drink
Thursday DAY 10 Green Veggie Day	Cloud or Microwave Bread with **1 TABLE SPOON OF BUTTER ONLY**	Any pepper soup of your choice	Green Vegetable such as Ugwu or Spinach with 2 tablespoons of Butter or coconut oil	Walk minimun 5,000 Steps Drink 8 glasses of water or Flat Belly Detox Drink
Friday DAY 11	2 Boiled eggs and 1 sausage	Chicken,Fish or Turkey cooked any way you want with 1 cup GREEN Veggies	1 cucumber	Walk minimun 5,000 Steps Drink 8 glasses of water or Flat Belly Detox Drink

3 WEEKS WEIGHTLOSS MEAL PLAN

Saturday **DAY 12** **ZERO CARB**	 2 Tins of Sardine or Tuna fried in butter or coconut oil	 Chicken and Mayo	 Suya or Grilled Fish	Walk minimun 7,000 Steps Drink 8 glasses of water or Flat Belly Detox Drink
Sunday **DAY 13**	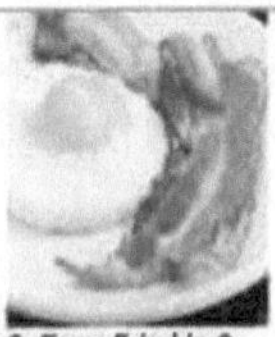 2 Eggs Fried in 2 tablespoon of Butter, palm oil or coconut oil and bacon.	 Asun /Nkwobi or Isi Ewu	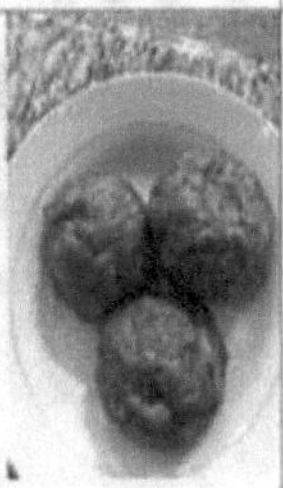 Its Saturday Try something new Fish or Chicken fritters	Drink 8 glasses of water or Flat Belly Detox Drink
Monday **DAY 14** **Zero Carb Day**	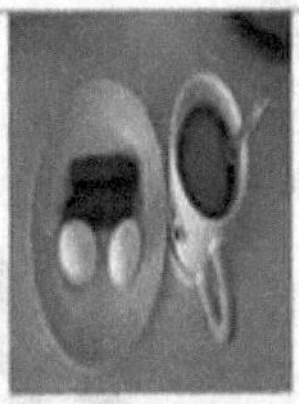 Max 3 boiled eggs with 1 sausage	 Fish or Chicken with Mayonnaise	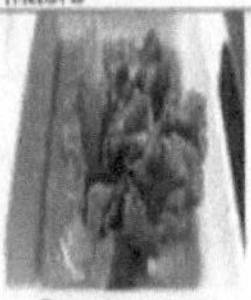 Goat meat or Fish pepper soup	Walk minimun 5,000 Steps Drink 8 glasses of water or Flat Belly Detox Drink
Tuesday **Day 15**				Walk minimun 5,000 Steps Drink 8 glasses of water or Flat

3 WEEKS WEIGHTLOSS MEAL PLAN

Saturday Day 19 Zero Carb Day	 2 Fried eggs with 2 Sausage	 Isi - Ewu, Nkwobi or Asun	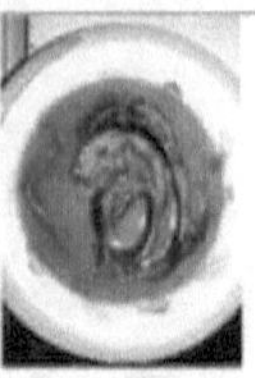 Fish Peppersoup	
Sunday Day 20 Zero Carb Day	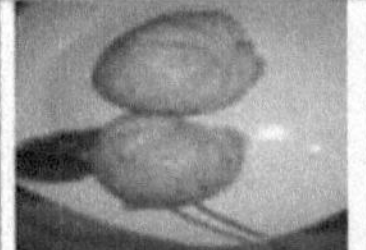 Egg or Chicken Moi moi	 Organ Meat Peppersoup	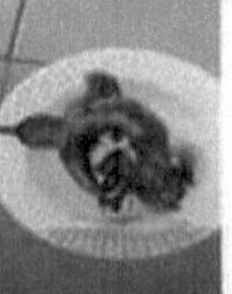 Dried or Fried Fish	Walk minimun 7,000 Steps

Drink 8 glasses of water or Flat Belly Detox Drink |

THE KETOGENIC DIARY

www.ingramcontent.com/pod-product-compliance
Lightning Source LLC
Chambersburg PA
CBHW031242250726
48655CB00005B/2052